Joan of Arc

Harold Nottridge

Illustrations by Angus McBride

The Bookwright Press
New York · 1988

Great Lives

Beethoven
Louis Braille
Captain Cook
Marie Curie
Einstein
Queen Elizabeth I
Queen Elizabeth II
Anne Frank
Gandhi
Joan of Arc
Helen Keller

John F. Kennedy
Martin Luther King, Jr.
John Lennon
Ferdinand Magellan
Karl Marx
Mozart
Napoleon
Florence Nightingale
Elvis Presley
William Shakespeare
Mother Teresa

Title page: A stained glass window of Joan's
martyrdom in Domrémy Church.

First published in the
United States in 1988 by
The Bookwright Press
387 Park Avenue South
New York NY 10016

First published in 1987 by
Wayland (Publishers) Limited
61 Western Road, Hove
East Sussex BN3 1JD, England

© Copyright 1987 Wayland (Publishers) Limited

ISBN 0–531–18177–4

Library of Congress Catalog Card Number: 87–71056

Phototypeset by Kalligraphics Limited, Redhill, Surrey
Printed in Italy by G. Canale & C.S.p.A., Turin

Contents

C. 1

The Maid of France

During the fifteenth century a girl called Joan was born into a farmer's family in Lorraine, France. Her life was short but her influence was to last for hundreds of years after her death. So much so that during World War II, 1939–45, the French people who were resisting the German occupation adopted a symbol to remind them of her – the double cross of Lorraine (the coat of arms of the Dukes of Lorraine).

Artists have created images of Joan as they thought she was. For some she was a peasant girl, for others a general in armor on horseback. For others again a

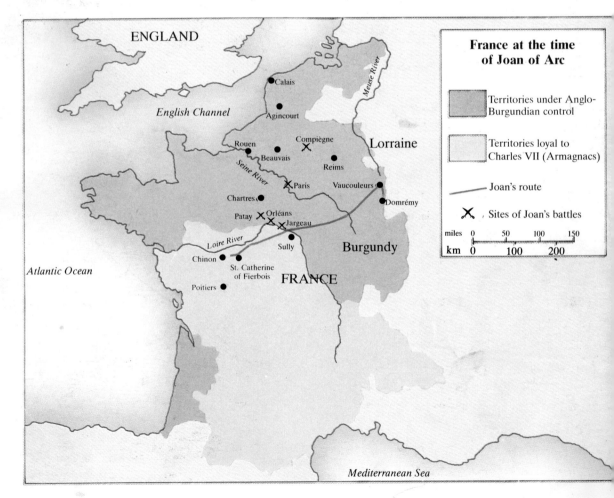

France at the time of Joan of Arc

- Territories under Anglo-Burgundian control
- Territories loyal to Charles VII (Armagnacs)
- Joan's route
- X Sites of Joan's battles

A contemporary painting of Joan (right), the Virgin Mary (center), and Saint Michael (left).

kindly girl who shed many tears over human suffering. A few have tried to paint her as a saint who could see things invisible to the majority of people.

She had a remarkable personality. She could not read or write, but could defend her thoughts and actions against subtle questions by learned men. "There are more things in God's book than in yours," she once answered a scholar. She was able to hearten discouraged people and give them the will to fight once more against their foes. She could make others believe in themselves, perhaps because she had an unshakable belief that she was to save France.

Documents tell us that Joan was dark-haired, very strong and courageous. She appeared at times to be able to communicate with a deeper more spiritual world than ours. We do not know exactly what that power was – only that this girl from Lorraine was to become the heroine of France and occupy a unique position in history.

This statue of Joan of Arc in Orléans is one of the many national monuments to her name.

Life in Domrémy

Joan came from Domrémy, a small remote village near the Meuse River. At that time England and France were bitter enemies in the Hundred Years' War. France itself was divided into two parts. One part was under the control of the Armagnacs who had a royal heir of their own, the Dauphin. The other part was ruled by the Burgundians who, at that time, helped the English invaders. The Domrémy villagers lived in an area of France where boundaries were disputed. These were lawless times in which the villagers were constantly raided by wandering bandits.

Jacques d'Arc, Joan's father, was an important person in the village. He was a stern and honest man who expected that his daughter would marry a farmer. His wife Isabelle was a proud, religious woman. Their life was a hard one, tied to the routine of the seasons. Yet there were holy days that were breaks from work when the children would hang flowers on the Fairies' Tree and dance happily beneath its branches, as the fairies were said to have done.

These were superstitious

The room in Domrémy in which Joan was born.

times. If someone was stricken by an unknown disease it was believed that a witch had cast a spell over that person. Witches could be burned for such happenings. Moreover, if people did not believe in what the Church said, they were considered to be heretics, for which the penalty was burning.

Among legends and sayings there was a prophecy that France would be saved by a girl dressed in men's clothing who would come from an oak forest in Lorraine.

This was the country in which Joan of Arc was born.

Villagers in Domrémy putting out fires after an attack by bandits.

The voices and the visions

Joan of Arc was one of five children. Like most village children she could not read or write, and her experience of life was limited to the village. However, her mother had taught her prayers and told her stories about the saints. Joan was deeply religious and would pray for hours in the church. She was a kind girl, comforting those who were ill. It was said that wild birds would feed readily out of her hands.

At the age of thirteen she had a remarkable experience. One

At the age of thirteen, Joan saw a great bright light and heard voices.

summer day, when she was in her father's garden, she heard a voice, although no one was nearby. At the same time she saw a great, bright light. Although at first fearful, she believed that the voice came from God because it told her to pray, to go to church and live a good life. Later, after other occasions when she heard several voices, she decided that they were the voices of angels.

Joan began to hear the voices frequently. She often went to a tiny chapel in the woods just outside Domrémy. There Joan could feel that she was in the presence of God.

Years passed by. Joan now also began to see visions, mainly of three saints – St. Michael the Archangel, St. Catherine and St. Margaret. The angels told her she must lead the French armies to victory at Orléans where the English were besieging the city. She must also see that Charles the Dauphin was crowned King of France and she must win back Paris from the English and Burgundians. She had only one year in which to do this.

Joan began to have visions from God telling her she must save France.

Joan leaves home

At about this time an English commander, who was going to Orléans with a supply of herrings for the English besiegers, was attacked by a much larger French force, which he managed to beat off. The French despaired at being overrun by the English.

Joan's voices gave her guidance. They told her to go to Robert de Baudricourt, Captain of Vaucouleurs, near Domrémy. Luckily she had a relative there, Durand Lassois, with whom she could stay. She did not dare tell her parents that her mission was to save France. She managed to get an audience with de Baudricourt, a tough soldier, who

The castle at Chinon, where the Dauphin held court.

listened with astonishment when this girl, in her patched, red woolen dress, said that she would save France and that he must help her to go to Charles, the Dauphin. At first de Baudricourt dismissed her.

Joan was strong-willed. She returned later to plead with de Baudricourt and this time found him ready to hear her. He now thought that if the French soldiers believed Joan was sent from Heaven to save France it might give them courage. Joan cut her hair short and put on men's clothing, since this might prevent her from being attacked when passing through enemy territory. De Baudricourt gave her an escort and she set off for Chinon where the Dauphin held court. It was a perilous winter journey partly through lands under Burgundian control. They traveled by night to avoid the enemy and slept where they could. Joan's endurance was as great as that of her companions.

In March they arrived at the town of Chinon and the great castle occupied by the Dauphin.

Joan, dressed as a man, traveled by night to Chinon.

Joan meets the Dauphin

Charles the Dauphin, uncrowned King of France, was a cowardly young man who preferred not to fight. The King had heard of the courage of Joan, but hesitated before finally agreeing to see her. His meeting with Joan was a remarkable occasion. The great hall of the castle was crowded with people all eager to see her. To test her, the King had dressed in courtiers' clothes. But Joan immediately recognized that he was the King. She bowed low and said, "Gentle Dauphin, I am Joan the Maid. The King of Heaven sends me with this message. You shall be crowned in Reims, and I will raise the siege of Orléans, for it is God's will that the English shall leave France." They then had a private talk together and she revealed a "sign" to him. What she said is unknown but from that moment the Dauphin began to trust her. It is clear that Joan had a genuine affection for her King.

Charles's counselors did not entirely accept Joan and persuaded him to send her to Poitiers where scholars could test her claim and discover whether she came from God or the Devil. She answered them intelligently and frankly. Once she lost her temper and told them she had not come to Poitiers to waste time in giving them proof of her mission but to raise the siege of Orléans. In the end the scholars, led by Regnault of Chartres, decided that the King could have the girl's help and advised that she should be sent to Orléans.

Below *Joan arriving at Chinon.*

Below *Joan recognized the Dauphin even though he was dressed as a courtier.*

A leader of warriors

A suit of plate armor and some helmets were made for Joan. She often preferred a steel cap, which left her face uncovered so that her troops could recognize her. In battle she wore a basinet, a type of helmet fitted with a movable visor. The visor had holes through which she could breathe and see. Her armor weighed over fifty pounds. She was very proud of her standard and carried it into battle to be a rallying point for the French.

Joan had a great, black charger, but it was a spirited and restive horse that she could not mount. She told the soldiers to take it to the cross in front of the neighboring church. They did so and the horse returned quietly and caused no further trouble.

When it came to equipping Joan with a sword she simply said "The sword that I will use will be found hidden behind the altar of the church of St. Catherine of Fierbois." She had never been there, but when the people went to see if they could find the sword sure enough it was there behind the altar.

Joan became friends with the military leaders. Alençon, a fine nobleman whom she greatly liked, helped her to become a superb horsewoman. Joan was concerned for her soldiers and liked them to attend Mass regularly and to refrain from drunkenness. Her magnetic personality made her popular both with her army and with the common people who would reverently kneel down before her.

A fifteenth-century woodcut showing Joan in her armor.

Right *Joan was a popular leader who inspired her soldiers.*

Orléans – the turning point

The English had besieged Orléans for months and had even built forts around it. The French troops, huddled behind the city walls, were afraid, even though they outnumbered the English. Joan's task was to inspire her countrymen to drive out the invaders. She planned to get food through to the hungry citizens and to lead her men to victory over the English.

Provision barges were sent up the river. They were delayed by unfavorable winds, but Joan predicted that the winds would change and so they did. The barges reached Orléans to the joy of its inhabitants who began almost to worship Joan. The French then attacked the English forts. Joan was always at the front with her standard, encouraging her troops with her bravery and enthusiasm. The English were amazed to see a

Joan courageously led her troops to defeat the English at Orléans.

woman leading the fighting. They shouted vile insults at her that made her weep. They threatened to burn her if they captured her.

Inspired by her courage the French regained all the forts except Les Tourelles. A fierce battle raged there and an arrow struck Joan in the neck. She had to leave the battlefield for a few hours rest. She went into a vineyard and prayed to God to give her strength. When she returned to the battle the French were retreating. But they saw her standard, regained their courage and charged the fort again. The English refused to surrender to a woman and ran back onto the burning drawbridge, which fell down under them. They were thrown into the moat where, weighed down by their armor, they drowned. It was a glorious victory for Joan and the French. The city of Orléans once more belonged to France.

Weeks of victory

When the people of Orléans saw the besiegers leave defeated, they knew that Joan had won a moral as well as a physical victory. She had defeated battle-hardened English soldiers. Joan had gained Orléans for the Dauphin. Now she wanted him to be crowned at Reims. To do this the French army would have to advance across land that was under the control of the English and the Burgundians. The Dauphin's advisers wanted to delay an advance and spent weeks in

On entering Orléans Joan and her men received a glorious welcome.

The standard, flag and banner that were carried by Joan of Arc.

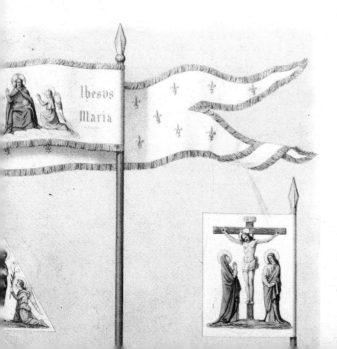

useless talks in the council. Joan despaired at the wasted time. She went to see Charles and begged him not to delay. Her impatience spurred him on. A new French army was gathered to attack strongholds in the Loire valley. Joan led her men to the important town of Jargeau, which they captured.

Eventually they came across a large English army near Patay. The English were surprised and the French quickly won the battle with the loss of many Englishmen but very few Frenchmen. The battle of Patay was a great encouragement for the French as it was the first big battle they had won so far. It also opened up the road to Reims.

For Joan battles were also human tragedies. She cried bitterly over the English soldiers who had died and said prayers for their souls. She was once seen holding the head of a wounded English soldier, listening to him confessing his sins. She comforted him while he died. Sometimes, out of pity, she would even forbid her troops to pursue a beaten enemy. It was a sign of her compassion that she never used her sword to kill anyone.

Joan showed her compassion by comforting a dying Englishman.

Triumph and failure

The King's coronation at Reims was held on a beautiful summer day. It was the peak of Joan's triumph. Clad in gleaming armor, with a cloak of red and gold over her shoulders and her standard unfurled, she proudly stood close to the King.

The King was anointed with holy oil and was crowned before the assembly. Among the crowd was Joan's father. He watched his daughter kneel and saw her whisper tearfully. "You are the true King and lord over the land of France." As a reward of her services, Charles granted the Domrémy villagers freedom from paying taxes and also ennobled her family.

But after the coronation things began going badly for Joan. The King, instead of pressing on fast to Paris, made treaties with the Duke of Burgundy who did not want to give up that city. While they delayed, a new English army was crossing the Channel to reach France.

Paris, a city under Burgundian control, was the key to French victory over the English. An assault was planned, but an event occurred that cast gloom over Joan's troops. She was driving women camp followers away and as she struck one with

The coronation of Charles the Dauphin at Reims.

the flat of her sword the blade broke. It was the holy sword of St. Catherine and the troops thought that its snapping was a bad omen. Many thought Joan had lost her power.

The attack on Paris began. While testing the depths of the moat an arrow wounded Joan in the leg. Seeing her wounded, the soldiers lost courage and attacked Paris only half-heartedly. The attack failed and the French retreated.

Joan besieged Paris, but the attack failed and the French retreated.

The French soldiers lost courage when they saw that Joan was injured.

Captivity

In a skirmish near Compiègne the Burgundians captured Joan. Charles did nothing – perhaps because he now wanted to get rid of her. Joan made frantic attempts to escape. She even jumped down from a tower sixty-five feet high. She was unhurt but was recaptured. After some months the Burgundians, who wanted money, sold her to the English for a large sum.

On Christmas day, 1430, the English triumphantly led Joan into Rouen castle. The soldiers waited jubilantly for the girl they considered to be the hated witch whose spells had brought such

The old houses of Rouen dating back to the fifteenth century.

A statue of Joan at Compiègne, where she was captured.

humiliation upon their armies. They saw a small woman in very shabby men's clothing, her hands tied behind her back. The Burgundians had treated her respectfully and she had not even worn manacles. The English wanted to make sure that she would not escape. The soldiers seized Joan, and to her surprise and horror, her feet and hands were shackled firmly together with heavy iron chains, as though she were a common criminal.

Joan protested. She was told she would be better treated if she gave her word not to escape. She refused, believing that she had a right to try to escape if she could.

Joan, imprisoned in Rouen castle, with her hands and feet in chains.

She bravely chose to remain chained, for months, rather than give up that right.

She was imprisoned in a damp, cold cell. Day and night she was watched by the roughest English soldiers who tormented and insulted her. Chained always by her hands and feet to a huge beam, she had to await her inevitable fate. The English would burn her alive at the stake.

The trial of Joan

An ecclesiastical court tried Joan for heresy. But there was little hope for Joan. A few honest men declared the trial to be unjust, but her judges were mainly under the influence of the ruthless Bishop Cauchon, a friend of the English and an enemy of Charles. Joan had no lawyer to defend her. For months the judges questioned her and tried to trap her into saying something that would prove she was a heretic. She answered intelligently.

Joan's judges were medieval clergy and they regarded her as a demon who had called up evil spirits. They questioned her often about her voices and visions, which they claimed challenged the authority of the Church. Joan remained convinced of the truth of her voices, even when she was threatened with torture.

In May she was taken to the cemetery where a stake was ready and was told that she

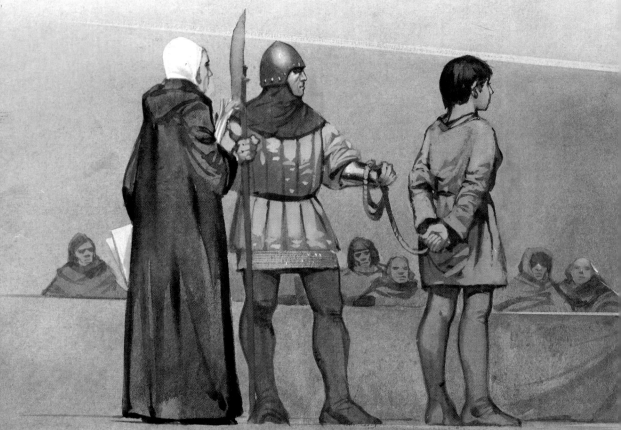

would be burned if she did not accept that the Church was right. Worn out, ill and afraid of death by fire she retracted her former statements. She denied that she had ever heard voices and agreed to wear women's clothing as part of her willingness to accept the teachings of the Church.

Two days later Cauchon found Joan again in men's clothing. She also said that she could hear her voices and what they said was true. These were acts of disobedience to the Church and Joan was doomed. The court declared her to be a relapsed heretic and recommended that she should be given over to secular justice for punishment. The English were delighted, for now they could execute her.

Joan was brought before a court and tried for heresy.

The last hours

Early in the morning of May 30, 1431, Joan was told that she must die. She cried piteously and said to Cauchon, "Bishop, I die through you." Her head was shaved and she was dressed in a woman's black robe and led to the Old Market in Rouen where a high scaffold awaited her. While she listened to the sermon she knelt, weeping and praying. The Bishop excommunicated her. She begged for a cross and an English soldier, moved by her tears, made one of wood. She asked for a crucifix to be held before her eyes as she died and some sympathetic priests brought one to her.

The English soldiers dragged her to the scaffold. As she mounted it and saw the city below she cried, "Rouen, Rouen, I fear that you will suffer for my death." They chained her to the stake and crowned her head with a tall, paper cap on which was written, "Heretic, relapsed, apostate, idolatress." Even in that last hour her love for the King persisted, for she said, "What I have done, well or ill, the King had no share in it, not by him was I advised." A brave friar mounted the scaffold and stood there praying with her until the flames drove him down. Then he remained below holding up the crucifix toward her. He testified afterward that she had called upon her saints and cried as she died, "My voices have not deceived me." Her last words were "Jesus, Jesus."

After she had died, an Englishman, who had watched the burning, muttered in horror to those around him, "We are lost for we have burned a saint."

Bishop Cauchon told Joan that she had been found guilty.

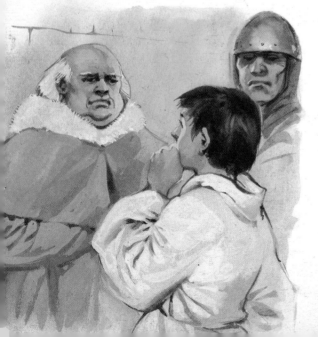

Right *Joan was burned at the stake as a heretic in Rouen.*

Vindication and canonization

Joan was dead. The English with relief threw her ashes into the river. Now they could fight the French without fear of the witch. They hoped that their young King, Henry VI, would be crowned King of France in Reims. The people of Reims would not allow this and Henry was crowned in Paris. It was an empty act. The Duke of Burgundy made peace with Charles whose armies gradually pushed the English out of France. After a few years only Calais remained in the hands of the English. Joan's prophecies had come true.

Twenty years after Joan's death, Charles ordered an

At the new trial Joan's mother claimed that Joan had been innocent.

Notre Dame in Paris, in which the Rehabilitation was held.

inquiry into the truth about Joan's trial. This new trial, called the Rehabilitation, produced evidence from many witnesses. In November, 1450, there was a moving event in the church of Notre Dame in Paris where an aged woman appeared. She was Joan's mother, presenting her claim that Joan had been unjustly tried and punished. Finally on July 7, 1456, the court said that the sentence passed on Joan twenty-five years before was without force. Joan was declared innocent.

Over four hundred years after her death Joan was regarded as the national heroine of France. In the nineteenth century a movement grew demanding that Joan should be considered as a saint. After years of inquiry Joan was canonized in 1920. She became a saint not because of her achievement as the savior of France or as a military general, but for the virtue of her life and her faithfulness to the voice of God. A celebrated French writer said of Joan, "She was entirely human and never was humanity greater."

A stained glass window of Joan and the Angel in Domrémy Church.

Important dates

1337–
1475 The Hundred Years' War.
1412 Birth of Joan of Arc.
1415 Defeat of the French at Agincourt by Henry V of England.
1424 Joan first hears her voices.
1428 Joan's first visit to de Baudricourt at Vaucouleurs.
1429 Second visit to Vaucouleurs.
1429 The English defeat the French at the "Battle of the Herrings."
1429 Joan leaves Vaucouleurs for Chinon.
1429 (March) The Dauphin receives Joan at Chinon.
1429 Joan is tested by scholars at Poitiers.
1429 Joan arrives in Orléans.

1429 Capture of Jargeau.
1429 Battle of Patay. The English are heavily defeated.
1429 (July 17) Charles is crowned at Reims.
1429 The French attack on Paris fails.
1430 (May 23) Joan is captured at Compiegne by the Burgundians.
1430–
31   (December 25 to May 30) Joan is imprisoned in Rouen castle.
1431 (January 9) Her trial begins.
1431 (May 24) The recantation.
1431 (May 30) Joan is burned at the stake.
1456 (July 7) Joan is declared innocent.
1920 (May 16) Joan is canonized.

Glossary

Anointing   Applying oil as part of a religious ceremony.

Besiege   To attempt to capture a town or castle by surrounding it.

Canonize   To declare formally that someone is a saint.

Coronation   The ceremony of crowning a king or queen.

Dauphin   The eldest son of the King of France.

Ecclesiastical   Of the Church or clergy.

Excommunicate   To cut off from membership in the Church.

Heresy   A belief different from the accepted beliefs of the Church.

Moat   A trench, usually filled with water, surrounding a castle or fort.

Recant   To withdraw formally in public an opinion once held.

Relapse   To fall back into a former state, or error.

Retract   To withdraw or take back an opinion.

Scaffold   A raised platform on which criminals and heretics were put to death.

Secular   Not religious or sacred.

Treaty   An agreement between nations.

Truce   A halt to fighting between armies.

Books to read

Her Way: A Guide to Biographies of Women for Young People 2nd edition by Mary-Ellen K. Siegel. American Library Association, 1984.

Joan of Arc by Maurice Boutet de Monvel. Reprint of 1897 edition. Viking, 1980.

Joan of Arc by Anne Nicholson. Coach House, 1961.

Joan of Arc by Catherine Storr. Raintree Publishers, 1985.

Joan of Arc by Susan Banfield (part of the series World Leaders: Past and Present). Chelsea House, 1985.

Joan of Arc: The Brave Soldier by Dolores Ready. Winston Press, 1975.

Joan of Arc: The Image of Female Heroism by Marina Warner. Random House, 1982.

Portraits of Courageous Women by Ardis O. Higgins. Halls of Ivy, 1978.

Wind and Shadows. Compiled and published by The Daughters of Saint Paul.

Picture credits

Mary Evans Picture Library 5, 13, 18, 20, 21; French Government Tourist Office 6; The Mansell Collection 18; Ronald Sheridan's Photo-Library *title page*, 14, 22 (both), 29; John Topham Picture Library 10; Malcolm Walker 4; ZEFA Picture Library 5, 29.

Index